TITLE PAGE:

STOCK MARKET TECHNIQUE:

A COMPLETE BEGINNER'S GUIDE. FROM ZERO EXPERIENCE TO BECOMING A PROFESSIONAL STOCK INVESTOR.

Discover The Secrets Of

Jack Bogle stock market strategy

Warren Buffett method of stock selection

Peter Lynch Stock Market Strategy

Benjamin Graham Stock Market Strategy

USER FRIENDLY.

All rights reserved. No part of this publication may be reproduced, distributed or transmitted in any form or by any means, including photocopying, recording or other electronic or mechanical methods, without the prior written permission of the publisher, except in the case of brief quotations embodied in critical reviews and certain other non-commercial uses permitted by copyright law © (ROY H. JONES), (2024).

TABLE OF CONTENTS

AN INTRODUCTION TO STOCK MARKET	4
GETTING STARTED WITH STOCK MARKET:	6
The Fundamentals of Investing: Creating Long-Term Value while Managing Risk	36
Jack Bogle stock market strategy	38
Warren Buffett method of stock selection	41
Peter Lynch Stock Market Strategy:	45
Benjamin Graham Stock Market Strategy	47
Gaining profits via Exchange-Traded Funds (ETFs):	49
Dividend stocks: A Way to Generate Passive Income	52
PIEs and Value Investing:	55
Investing in Growth Stocks to Gain Profit:	58
Using initial public offerings (IPOs) to generate revenue	61
Opportunities and Market Capitalization	64
Ten costly Mistakes Beginners Make:	67
IDEAL TIMING FOR STOCK BUYING:	71
WHEN TO SALE A STOCK:	73
THE SECRET METHODS TO MAKE MONEY FROM UNPROGRESSIVE STOCK	75
In summary:	78

AN INTRODUCTION TO STOCK MARKET

Comprehending the Stock Market: The stock market is a vibrant and intricate financial marketplace where people and institutions transact ownership shares in publicly listed corporations. As a means of enabling businesses to acquire capital and offering investors the chance to increase their wealth, it is an essential part of the global economy.

How to Operate It

The fundamental idea behind supply and demand drives the stock market. A company's stock, which represents a portion of the ownership share in that business, is purchased by investors who see growth and profitability potential in the enterprise. Investors may, on the other hand, sell a company's stock if they are skeptical or concerned about its future.

Key players

The stock market is populated by several important players:

1. Companies: To generate money for a variety of goals, including growing their business, acquiring new technology, or paying off debt, they issue stocks.

2. Investors: These encompass persons, establishments, and funds engaged in the purchase and sale of stocks. Through dividends (a portion of the company's profits) and capital appreciation (an increase in the value of the stock), they hope to generate returns.

3. Dealers and Brokers:

Brokers assist buyers and sellers in stock transactions in exchange for commissions or other fees. Exchanges that offer the platforms for buying and selling stocks are the New York Stock Exchange (NYSE) and NASDAQ.

4. Regulators: Organizations that keep an eye on the stock market to safeguard investors' interests, uphold market integrity, and promote fair and transparent trading procedures include the Securities and Exchange Commission (SEC).

Indexes of the Stock Market

In order to assess the overall performance of the market, analysts frequently monitor stock market indices such as the NASDAQ Composite, S&P 500, and Dow Jones Industrial Average (DJIA). These indices offer insights into market patterns and investor sentiment by representing baskets of equities from different industries.

Perils and Benefits
Potential benefits of stock market investing include portfolio diversification, dividends, and capital gains. But there are hazards associated with it as well, such as fluctuations in the market, dangers unique to a company, recessions, and changes in regulations. Thorough research, portfolio diversification, consideration of risk tolerance and investing objectives are all necessary for investors.

In conclusion:
An essential function of the stock market in the global economy is to facilitate capital raising for businesses and to allow investors to partake in wealth creation. For anyone trying to navigate this fascinating yet tough financial landscape, it is imperative to understand its basics, main players, indexes, risks, and rewards.

GETTING STARTED WITH STOCK MARKET:

Long-term wealth accumulation through stock investments can be quite effective.
Considering the following step-by-step instructions:

Step 1:

Know Your Financial Objectives

Determine your financial status and establish specific investment goals before you enter the stock market. Choose your investing time horizon, risk tolerance, and goals (such as retirement savings, home ownership, or college funding). Clarity in financial goals helps you make well-informed decisions that are consistent with your dreams and serves as a road map for your investing journey. Consider the following important factors:

1. Comparing short- and long-term objectives
Expenses or goals that you hope to accomplish in the next few years, including vacation savings, vehicle purchase, or emergency fund building, are examples of short-term goals. Investment liquidity and stability are frequently necessary to achieve short-term objectives.
Long- Range Objectives: A child's education, retirement preparation, or home ownership are examples of long-term aspirations that span several years or decades. Strategic investing techniques can leverage compounding and growth potential when they are based on long-term goals.

2. The Ability to Take Risks
Find out how comfortable you are with possible losses on your investments by doing a risk assessment. A person's age, age stability, investment experience, and mental attitude toward risk are all factors that affect their risk tolerance. Your portfolio's investment mix might be influenced by your understanding of risk tolerance.

3. Period of Investment

It is important to think about the duration of your investment, which might vary from less than three years to over 10 years. Longer investing horizons frequently permit more aggressive techniques, whilst shorter horizons could necessitate a more cautious approach to preserve money.

The fourth is financial goals

Establish precise monetary targets that correspond with your objectives, such as:

Provisions for Retirement: Based on your estimated expenses, age at retirement, and sources of income (such as investments, Social Security, and pensions), calculate how much you need to save for retirement.

- Education Financing: Compute how much it will cost you, your kids, or your dependents to attend school. To reach education finance targets, investigate investment alternatives and college savings plans (such as 529 plans).
- Purchasing a home: Determine the monthly housing expenses, down payment, and mortgage affordability. If you want to save money for a down payment, think about investing.
- Manage Your Debt: Make paying off high-interest loans and credit cards your top priority. Create a plan to pay off debt while saving money for other objectives.

Establish an emergency fund in order to pay for unforeseen costs or interruptions in income. Based on monthly spending and risk considerations, establish the right size of emergency fund.

5. Lifestyle Things to Take Into Account

Think about the things that are important to you financially and in terms of your lifestyle, such as legacy planning, travel, hobbies, and charitable donations. A rewarding and long-lasting financial strategy is the result of balancing your lifestyle and investing choices.

6. Assess and Modify

Evaluate and modify your financial objectives on a regular basis in response to changes in your life. To make sure that your investment plan is still in line with your changing requirements and goals, periodically reevaluate your risk tolerance, time horizon for investments, and goals.

In summary:
A key component of successful investing is knowing your financial objectives. You may create an all-encompassing financial plan and make well-informed investment decisions that are specific to your goals and circumstances by setting clear goals, evaluating your risk tolerance, taking investing timelines into account, and prioritizing your financial needs.

Step 2: Learn Everything You Can About Stocks

A fundamental understanding of the various stock kinds, important financial measures, fundamental analytical methods, and the workings of the stock market is necessary for stock investing. When learning about stocks, take into account the following important factors:

1. How Stocks Operate
Begin by understanding the fundamentals of how stocks work:
• Ownership: Stocks stand for shares of a company's ownership. Upon purchasing stocks, you assume a portion of the company's ownership and are liable for both its gains and losses.
• Market dynamics: Supply and demand, mood of the market, economic conditions, business success, and industry trends all affect stock prices.
• Dividends and Capital Gains: A stock's dividends, which are a portion of the profits given to owners, and capital gains, which are an increase in the stock's value over time, are two ways that stocks might yield returns.

2. Kinds of Stocks
Recognize the various stock options available.

- Common Stocks: These are the most commonly traded stocks, with the possibility for dividends and capital growth along with ownership rights.
- Preferred Stocks: They are entitled to fixed dividends and have precedence over common stockholders when it comes to dividend payments and liquidation assets.

3. Crucial Finance Measures

Become knowledgeable about the key financial indicators used to assess stocks:

In order to determine a company's valuation in relation to earnings, the Price-to-Earnings (P/E) Ratio compares the stock price to earnings per share.
- Earnings Per Share (EPS): computed by dividing net earnings by the number of outstanding shares to determine a company's profitability.
- Dividend Yield: Shows how the stock price and annual dividend income compare, offering information on dividend returns.

Market capitalization is the process of multiplying a company's stock price by the number of outstanding shares to get its overall market worth.

4. Basic Examination

To evaluate a company's financial standing and investment prospects, become knowledgeable about fundamental research techniques:

Income statements, balance sheets, and cash flow statements should all be analyzed in order to assess revenue, costs, assets, liabilities, and cash flows.
- Business Model: Recognize the market position, development potential, industry, competitive advantages, and hazards specific to the organization.
- Management Team: Evaluate the team's experience, vision, and leadership within the organization.
- Industry and Economic Trends: Remain up to date on market dynamics, sector-specific trends, regulatory developments, and macroeconomic data that affect stock performance.

5. Techniques for Investing

Examine many methods to stock investing and investment strategies:
- Value Investing: Looks for cheap equities with solid foundations and room to expand.

- Growth Investing: Invests primarily in stocks of businesses with strong growth rates and bright future outlooks, frequently at premium prices.
- Income Investing: This strategy gives preference to equities that, for investors looking for consistent cash flow, offer stable income in the form of dividends.

6. Lifelong Learning

With the help of reliable sources, books, courses, seminars, and internet resources, stay current on financial news, market trends, investing methods, and industry advancements. Continue to learn new things and hone your investing techniques so that you can make wise choices.

In conclusion

A vital first step toward being a self-assured and profitable investor is learning about stocks. You may successfully navigate the stock market with knowledge and skill to meet your investing goals if you understand how stocks operate, the various types of stocks, important financial measures, fundamental analysis methodologies, investment strategies, and the importance of ongoing education.

Step 3: Open a brokerage account

Select a trustworthy brokerage company that suits your investing requirements and tastes. Examine elements including costs, account minimums, customer support, and research tools. Fill out the account opening form, including the required financial and personal details.

You can purchase and sell stocks, bonds, mutual funds, exchange-traded funds (ETFs), and other investment products using a brokerage account, which acts as your entry point into the stock market. What you should know before creating a brokerage account is as follows:

1. Select an Adequate Brokerage Company

For your investing journey, choosing the correct brokerage business is crucial. When selecting a brokerage, keep the following things in mind:

Charges and Commissions: Examine trade commissions, transaction fees, and account fees. Seek out brokers who offer prices that are reasonable and in line with your trading volume and investment amount.

Account Categories: Find out what kinds of accounts the brokerage offers: margin accounts, individual taxable accounts, education savings accounts (like 529 plans), retirement accounts (like Traditional IRAs and Roth IRAs), and retirement accounts.

Investing Choices: Examine the variety of financial products that are offered, such as futures, bonds, stocks, mutual funds, ETFs, and options. To fit your investing preferences, pick a brokerage that provides a wide range of options.

Study and Instruments: Examine the brokerage's trading platforms, market analysis tools, research tools, educational materials, and investment screening tools. Strong research skills can improve your ability to make investment decisions.

Client Assistance: Take into mind the level of customer support, timeliness, accessibility of support channels (such as phone, email, and live chat), and help with questions or problems pertaining to accounts.

2. Finish creating your account.

After selecting a brokerage, open a brokerage account by following these instructions:

Application Online: Most brokerages allow you to open an account online by providing financial facts (income, net worth), work information, investment experience, and personal information (name, address, Social Security number).

Recordings: Agree to Terms: Read over and accept the brokerage's terms and conditions, which include account agreements, risk disclosures, fee schedules, and regulatory disclosures. Prepare identification documents, such as a driver's license or passport issued by the government, proof of address (utility bill, bank statement), and tax identification number (SSN or TIN).

Options for Financing: Select the payment method for your account: wire transfer, bank transfer, electronic funds transfer (EFT), or check deposit. To fund your account, adhere to the guidelines supplied by the brokerage.

Check Information: Before submitting your application, make sure the information is correct. Verify account information, contact details, and funding instructions one more time.

3. Provide Funds for Your Account
Fund your brokerage account with the amount you plan to invest as soon as it's approved. Examine the following sources of funding:
Digital Transfers: Start automating transfers to and from your brokerage account and associated bank account. To ensure secure setup and processing of transfers, adhere to the brokerage's instructions.
Wire Transfers: Provide money by a wire transfer to have faster processing times; they are often accessible for bigger sums. Pay attention to any costs your bank or brokerage may charge for wire transfers.
Deposits with checks: If available, use mobile check deposit services or mail a physical check to fund your brokerage account. Give yourself time for the check to clear before gaining access to trade funds.

4. Look Through Account Features
Examine the features and capabilities your brokerage account offers after it has been funded.
Platform for Trading: Get acquainted with the trading platform of the brokerage, covering order entry, market data, charting tools, research reports, watchlists, and portfolio tracking.
Handling Accounts: To manage your account, access account statements, transaction history, tax forms (1099 forms, for example), account settings, and security measures (two-factor authentication, for example).
Use the brokerage's research tools, instructional materials, webinars, tutorials, and market insights to improve your understanding of investments and your ability to make decisions.
Customer Support: Keep your contact details handy and send questions about trade, technical difficulties, or account-related concerns to customer support.

5. Go Into Investment
You are prepared to begin investing in stocks and other securities after your brokerage account has been established and filled. Develop a diversified

portfolio, carry out due diligence, evaluate investment prospects, and execute trades in accordance with your investment plan and objectives.

In conclusion

Getting access to the stock market and starting your investing adventure both depend on opening a brokerage account. You can start creating a diverse portfolio and achieving your financial goals by selecting a reputable brokerage, finishing the account opening procedure, financing your account, learning about account features, and making strategic investment decisions.

Step 4: Proceed to Fund Your Account.

Put as much money as you feel comfortable investing into your brokerage account once it has been set up. Payments can be made into your account by cheque or electronic fund transfers.

The following is how you can pay money into your brokerage:

EFT or ACH electronic transfers

If you want to fund your account electronically, several brokerage firms provide services like Electronic Funds Transfer (EFT) and Automated Clearing House (ACH). It functions as follows:

Connect the Bank Account: Make sure your bank account and brokerage account are linked by logging in. The routing and account numbers for your bank must be provided.

Start the Transfer: Go to your brokerage account's website or app and select the financing or deposit area. Enter the desired transfer amount and select the electronic transfer option.

Check and Acfirm: Examine the account data and transfer details, including the amount. Set the procedure in motion by confirming the transfer.

Processing Time: Depending on the banking and brokerage processes involved, electronic transfers might take anywhere from one to three business days to finalize.

2. Transfers by wire

To finance your brokerage account more quickly or for greater sums, you can use a wire transfer. What you should be aware of is this.

Brokerage Instructions: Get the bank name, account number, routing number, and any further instructions or reference codes (if applicable) from your brokerage when transferring money.

Send the wire transfer instructions from the brokerage to your bank or other financial institution to start the process. Indicate the quantity that you want to move.

Verify the Transfer: Check the wire transfer's specifics, including any fees your bank may have assessed. Set the procedure in motion by confirming the transfer.

Processing Time: You can get funds in your brokerage account quickly because wire transfers are usually completed the same day or within one business day.

3. Deposits by check

By depositing a physical check, you can fill your brokerage account. It functions as follows:

To get instructions for making a deposit: To access the deposit or financing area, log into your brokerage account. Seek out guidelines for using mobile check deposit services or mailing checks in.

Get the Check Ready: Make sure your brokerage account is paid using a check. Ascertain that the check has your account number and any necessary instructions or endorsements.

Please mail the check to the address your brokerage has supplied if you are depositing it by mail. Bring the check along with any necessary papers or deposit slips.

Check Deposit on the Go: Using their mobile apps, certain brokerages provide mobile check deposit capabilities. To submit the check electronically for deposit, follow the instructions to take pictures of both the front and back.

Allow time for check clearing: Depending on the brokerage's policies and check processing procedures, check clearing can take anywhere from one to five business days.

4 Different Sources of Funding

Additional funding possibilities may be available to you based on your brokerage.
Move from Another Brokerage: To initiate an account transfer or an ACATS (Automated Customer Account Transfer Service) transfer, you must follow the brokerage's procedures.

Cash Deposits: Bank affiliations or physical branch facilities are two ways that certain brokerages may accept cash deposits. For information on available cash deposit methods, contact your brokerage.

Individual Retirement Account (IRA) Contributions: If you are funding an IRA, you are able to make direct contributions to the IRA account, subject to IRS requirements and yearly contribution limits.

5: Check and Get Money

The money in your brokerage account will be available to you once your funding method has been approved and processed by your brokerage. Afterward, you can use these funds to purchase bonds, mutual funds, equities, exchange-traded funds, and other investments in accordance with your investing goals and plan.

To sum up:
You can put funds into your brokerage account to begin investing. Funding your account is an easy process. For trading and investing purposes, make sure you follow your brokerage's instructions and give processing enough time, regardless of the funding method you select—electronic transfers, wire transfers, check deposits, or other.

Step 5: Examine Stocks

Before making an investment, thoroughly investigate possible stocks. Examine the company's finances, market trends, competitors' strategies, leadership group, and future growth potential. For information, consult corporate filings, analyst reports, and financial websites.
Here is a thorough how-to instruction for stock research:

1. Recognize the Organization

Business Model: To begin, ascertain the primary business operations, goods and services offered by the organization, as well as its target markets, competitive advantages, and sources of income.
Analyze the competitive landscape, market size, growth patterns, regulatory environment, and technical breakthroughs in the industry the company operates in.
SWOT Analysis: Use the SWOT analysis framework (Strengths, Weaknesses, Opportunities, Threats) to determine the main elements that impact a company's competitive position and overall performance.

2. Examination of Finances
Examine the company's income statement, balance sheet, and cash flow statement, among other financial statements. Examine operating efficiency, debt levels, cash flow trends, profitability margins, and revenue growth.
important financial ratios Determine and examine important financial ratios, including the debt-to-equity ratio, price-to-earnings (P/E), price-to-sales (P/S), return on equity (ROE), and earnings per share (EPS). These measures shed light on efficiency, profitability, leverage, and valuation.
Historical Performance: Analyze past financial results to spot trends, patterns, and long-term stability in performance.

3. Opportunities for Growth and Competitive Positioning
Market Share: Determine the company's place in the market in comparison to its rivals and assess its potential for growth.
Growth-Releasing Factors: Determine the main factors driving growth, including the introduction of new products, geographic expansion, shifts in consumer demand, innovation, and strategic alliances.
Competitive Analysis: Evaluate the company's strengths, shortcomings, and methods for differentiation in relation to benchmark businesses and peers in the industry.

4. Corporate Governance and Management

Management Team: Consider the CEO and other senior executives as well as the team's experience, performance history, style of leadership, and strategic vision.

Corporate Governance: Evaluate the company's transparency in financial reporting, shareholder rights, executive remuneration structure, and board makeup.

5. Analyst News and Reports; Analyst Suggestions: Examine recommendations and analyst reports from respectable analysts and financial institutions. Take into account price targets, analyst-provided qualitative observations, and consensus projections.

Current Affairs and Occurrences: Keep up with news about your company, its earnings, quarterly reports, new product releases, acquisitions and mergers, regulatory changes, and market trends that could affect the performance of your stocks.

6. Price and Valuation Objectives

Assessment Frameworks: To determine the stock's intrinsic value, apply valuation tools such discounted cash flow (DCF), price-to-earnings (P/E), price-to-book (P/B), and comparable company analysis (comps).

Price Objectives: Examine the price targets that analysts and financial institutions have set, taking into account their growth projections and methods of valuation.

7. Hazards and Points to Remember

Determine and evaluate any risks that could have an impact on the business, such as those related to the industry, the economy, competition, regulations, and the company itself.

Diversification: To lower concentration risk, think about portfolio diversification by purchasing a variety of companies from various sectors, industries, and geographical areas.

8. Utilizing Resources and Tools for Research

Financial Websites: To obtain company profiles, financial data, analyst reports, news updates, and stock screening capabilities, make use of financial websites, stock market platforms, and investment research tools.

Investment Newsletters: For professional insights, market analysis, and investment ideas, subscribe to respectable investment newsletters, industry publications, and financial periodicals.

9. Ongoing Observation and Evaluation

Monitor Performance: To keep abreast of developments that could affect investing decisions, keep a close eye on the company's performance as well as financial data, market circumstances, and industry trends.

Rebalancing a portfolio: Review and rebalance your stock holdings on a regular basis. Make adjustments to your investments based on shifting market conditions, risk tolerance, and financial goals.

In summary

A thorough examination of a company's fundamentals, growth prospects, competitive positioning, management caliber, valuation, risks, and market trends is necessary for effective stock research. Through comprehensive investigation and evaluation, investors can construct a well-organized portfolio that is in line with their investing objectives and risk tolerance.

Step 6: Selecting Your Investments

Choose stocks that fit your risk tolerance and portfolio diversification approach based on your research and investing objectives. Take into account elements including the company's growth potential, dividends, stability, and valuation.

Here is a thorough guide to investing selection:

1. Establish Your Investing Objectives

Decide whether your investing objectives are long-term (like saving for a vacation) or short-term (like planning for retirement or accumulating money).

Evaluate your level of comfort with probable losses and the volatility of investments by taking a look at your risk tolerance. Think about things like your age, your financial situation, your past investing experience, and your investment horizon.

2. Allocative Asset

Investing in a variety of asset classes, such as equities, bonds, cash equivalents, real estate, and alternative investments, can help you spread your risk and maximize rewards.

Trade-off between Risk and Return: To balance the risk-return profile of your portfolio, allocate assets according to their predicted returns, volatility, correlation, and benefits of diversification.

3. Various Investment Types

Depending on your objectives, risk tolerance, and investment horizon, take into consideration several investment types:

Stocks: Equities have the ability to increase in value and provide dividends, and they also symbolize ownership in businesses. Select companies according to industry trends, growth potential, company fundamentals, and valuation.

Bonds: Fixed-income instruments ensure a regular repayment of principal at maturity along with interest payments. Examine the credit ratings, rates, maturity dates, and bond kinds (such as corporate, municipal, and government bonds).

Mutual funds and exchange-traded funds (ETFs): These pooled investment vehicles provide diversification among a range of securities. Evaluate ETF features (such as expense ratios and tracking indices) and mutual fund categories (such as equities funds, bond funds, and index funds).

Property: To gain exposure to property markets, think about real estate investments like rental properties, REITs (Real Estate Investment Trusts), or real estate crowdfunding platforms.

Precious metals and commodities: Consider using precious metals and commodities (such as gold, silver, and oil) as diversification or inflation hedges.

4. Methods of Investment

worth investing focuses on basic analysis and long-term growth potential to find undervalued assets that are trading below their intrinsic worth.

When investing in growth, look for stocks of firms that have promising futures, cutting-edge business plans, a competitive edge, and rapid rates of earnings growth.

When it comes to investing, give priority to income-producing assets like bonds, preferred equities, dividend-paying companies, and income-oriented ETFs.

Index Investing: Take into consideration low-cost, passive index investing with index funds or exchange-traded funds (ETFs) that track market indices (such as the S&P 500 and NASDAQ).

Investing by sector and theme: Based on market trends and themes, consider investing in sectors such as technology, healthcare, or energy, or investing thematically in areas like developing markets, disruptive technologies, or environmental, social, and governance.

5. Research and Due Diligence for Investments

Comprehensive investigation and evaluation of possible investments should be done using fundamental analysis, taking into account aspects including cash flows, earnings growth, competitive positioning, industry trends, and management caliber.

Utilize technical analysis tools and charts to pinpoint price trends, levels of support and resistance, trading patterns, and market sentiment to determine the best times to enter and exit the market.

Assess the risks associated with investments, such as market risk, liquidity risk, interest rate risk, credit risk, geopolitical risk, and company-specific risk.

Historical Performance: Examine past results, volatility, risk-adjusted returns, and the consistency of investment performance over many market cycles.

6. Examine the Tax Consequences

Tax-Efficient Investing: When making investing decisions, keep taxes in mind. Think about capital gains management, tax-deferred accounts (401(k)s and IRAs), tax-loss harvesting, and tax-efficient investing techniques.

7. Keep an eye on and adjust

Routine Review: Keep a close eye on your portfolio to evaluate its performance, asset allocation, and degree of conformity with your financial objectives. Keep yourself updated on investment news, economic changes, and market trends.

Buying underperforming assets, selling overperforming ones, and modifying asset allocation are all ways to periodically rebalance your portfolio in order to minimize risk and maximize profits.

In conclusion

When selecting investments, you must carefully analyze your objectives, risk tolerance, asset allocation, investment kinds, tactics, tax implications, due diligence, and continuing oversight. You may create a well-structured portfolio that supports your financial goals and endures market swings by selecting investments holistically and diversifying across asset classes, industries, and methods.

Step 7: Place Your Orders

Place buy orders for the chosen stocks using your trading platform. Select between limit orders (executed at a defined price or better) and market orders (performed at the current market price).

Investors must comprehend various order types, pricing strategies, and execution techniques before placing orders in the stock market. This is a detailed guide explaining the ordering process:

Recognize the Types of Orders

Market Order: A market order directs your broker to purchase or sell shares at the going rate in the market. While they don't guarantee a certain price, market orders are executed instantly at the best available price.

Limit Order: A limit order indicates the highest price you are prepared to pay (buy limit order) or the lowest price you will take (sell limit order) for a stock. Although limit orders give you price control, they might not be carried out if the market price falls below your predetermined threshold.

A market order is triggered by a stop order, which is also referred to as a stop-loss order, when the stock price hits a predetermined stop price. By selling a stock at or below a set price, it helps reduce prospective losses.

A stop-limit order combines the functionality of a limit order with a stop order by setting off a limit order whenever the stock price reaches a predetermined stop price. Although it gives price control, if the market price is below the stop price, it might not execute.

2. Establish Ordering Guidelines

Quantity: In your order, indicate how many shares or units you wish to buy or sell.

Order Type: Market order, limit order, stop order, stop-limit order, or other order type should be selected depending on your trading strategy, price expectations, and risk management preferences.

Length: Select the length of the order, such as day order, which is good for the current trading day, or good 'til cancelled (GTC), which is active until it is executed or canceled.

3. Make Purchase Orders

Put in a market buy order with your broker to purchase a certain number of shares at the going rate. Orders to purchase goods on the market are filled right away at the best asking price.

Limit Purchase Order: Decide how much the highest price you will accept for a stock is (limit price). Only when the market price is at or below the limit price you have set will your buy order execute.

4. Issue Orders for Sale

Sell Market Order: Give your broker instructions to sell a certain number of shares at the going rate. Market sell orders are filled at the highest bid price right away.

Limit Sell Order: Decide how much less than the asking price you'll take to sell a stock. If the market price is at or higher than your designated limit price, your sell order will only be executed.

Order type, amount, price, and order duration are among the details you should examine after submitting an order. 5. Verify Order Status and Execution Confirmation.
Order Status: Use the order status or trade history area of your brokerage account to keep track of your order status (e.g., open, filled, cancelled, expired).
Execution: Observe the trade information, such as the execution price, timing, and any transaction fees or broker commissions, once your order has been executed.

6. Take into Account Market Conditions and Order Timing
Market Hours: Place orders for real-time execution at market prices between 9:30 AM and 4:00 PM Eastern Time, which is the usual trading hours for U.S. stock exchanges.
Trading After Hours: Certain brokerages provide extended or after-hours trading, which enables you to place orders outside of the typical trading hours. Keep in mind that during after-hours sessions, liquidity and price volatility may change.

7. Examine and Edit Purchases
Order Modifications: You can change or cancel open orders before they are filled if necessary. Modify the quantity, price, and duration of an order in response to shifting trading tactics or market conditions.
Order Book: Keep an eye on order book information, such as ask and bid prices, order volume, and order depth, to predict future price movements and assess the mood of the market.

8. Risk Control
Position Dimensions: Depending on your portfolio allocation, financial goals, and risk tolerance, determine the right position sizes.
Stop-Loss Orders: If you want to protect your assets from unfavorable price fluctuations and limit possible losses, think about utilizing stop-loss orders. Diversify your portfolio across asset classes, industries, and investing methods to minimize risk and maximize profits.

In conclusion

When placing an order in the stock market, one must carefully evaluate the market conditions, choose the appropriate order type, define the order parameters (quantity, price, duration), monitor the order's execution, and manage risk effectively. Investors may execute trades profitably and manage their portfolios by being aware of order types, timing, execution tactics, and order book dynamics.

Step8: Keep an Eye on Your Portfolio

Keep an eye on corporate news, market trends, and economic changes as you regularly analyze the performance of your stock portfolio. Reassess and modify your investments as necessary to maintain alignment with your objectives.

To efficiently monitor your portfolio, follow these crucial steps:

1. Decide on a monitoring frequency

Frequent Check-Ins: Establish weekly, biweekly, or monthly check-in times for monitoring your portfolio. You can stay up to date on market movements and portfolio dynamics by doing regular monitoring.

2. Monitor Your Performance

Compute the overall return of your investment portfolio, taking into account interest income, dividends, and capital gains. To determine the relative success of your portfolio, compare its performance to pertinent benchmarks (such as peer portfolios or market indices).

Risk-Adjusted Return: Use metrics such as the Sharpe ratio to assess risk-adjusted returns, as it gauges risk-adjusted performance in relation to volatility.

Asset Allocation: Keep an eye on the percentages of your assets to make sure they are allocated according to your goal. To keep the levels of asset allocation you want, frequently rebalance your portfolio.

3. Examine Particular Investments

Stocks and Funds: Assess the success of individual stocks, mutual funds, exchange-traded funds, and more investment vehicles within your portfolio. Evaluate the effects of news, dividends, price changes, and earnings reports on certain investments.

Fundamental Analysis: Keep up with the fundamental research on the stocks or mutual funds in your portfolio. To evaluate the quality of an investment, review the financial statements, cash flows, debt levels, industry trends, and earnings growth.

4. Track Trends in the Market

Economic Indicators: Remain aware of how macroeconomic indicators, such as GDP growth, inflation, and interest rates, may affect different asset classes, industries, and investing approaches.

Sector Rotation: Keep an eye on trends in the performance of each sector and think about redistributing funds among them in light of industry outlooks, economic cycles, and sector-specific variables.

Market Sentiment: To predict future trends and changes in the market, measure the mood using technical analysis indicators, investor sentiment indices, news, analyst reports, and sentiment indices for investors.

5. Assess the Risk of Exposure

Evaluate your portfolio's exposure to various risks, such as market, sector, interest rate, credit, currency, and geopolitical risks.

Make sure your portfolio is diversified across different asset classes, geographical areas, industries, and investment strategies in order to reduce the risk of concentration and improve risk-adjusted returns.

Stress Testing: Use scenario analysis or stress tests to assess how well a portfolio performs in volatile markets and pinpoint weak points.

6. Make a Portfolio Rebalance

Asset Allocation Rebalancing: To keep target asset allocation percentages, frequently rebalance your portfolio. Realign with your investment strategy by purchasing underperforming assets and selling overperforming ones.

Tax Considerations: When adjusting your portfolio, take taxes into account. Employ measures that minimize taxes, include capital gains management, asset placement optimization, and tax-loss harvesting.

7. Retain Knowledge and Education

Keep yourself informed on market news and updates, economic developments, financial news, and geopolitical events that could affect your portfolio.

Investment Research: To help you make wise selections, keep learning about and investigating asset classes, investment methods, market dynamics, and investment-related issues.

Review and Modify Your Investment Plans

Investment Objectives: Evaluate your time horizon, financial goals, risk tolerance, and investment objectives on a regular basis. Adapt your asset allocation and investing techniques as necessary in response to evolving conditions.

Lifestyle Changes: Adapt your investing strategy to your changing financial needs and objectives by taking into account life events such as marriage, children, retirement, and work changes.

9. Keep an eye on fees and costs

Examine the expenditure ratios as well as other fees associated with investments, transaction costs, and management fees. Reduce expenses whenever feasible to improve net investment returns.

10. Track and Document Your Progress

Portfolio Reports: For the purpose of following developments and filing taxes, keep track of transaction histories, trade confirmations, investment records, and portfolio performance reports.

Monitoring your progress toward financial objectives, retirement savings targets, financing for education, and other investment goals is called goal tracking. Goals and investment plans should be modified in light of successes and milestones.

In conclusion:
Rebalancing asset allocations, examining risks and market trends, evaluating individual assets, keeping track of performance metrics, modifying investing strategies, and recording progress are all part of portfolio monitoring. You may maximize investment results, efficiently manage risk, and work toward reaching your financial objectives by keeping a close eye on your portfolio and making well-informed decisions.

Step 9: Maintain Knowledge and Adjust

To effectively manage a portfolio in the ever-changing financial world of today, one must be aware and adjust to shifting market conditions. Here are some essential tactics to keep yourself updated and modify your investing strategy:

1. Lifelong Learning

Financial News and Updates: Use reliable news sources, financial websites, market analysis platforms, and market trends and indicators to stay up to date on geopolitical developments, market trends, and financial news.
study by Industry: To comprehend market trends, legislative modifications, technical developments, rivalry dynamics, and expansion prospects, conduct study tailored to your industry.
Learn more about investment concepts, techniques, and market insights by utilizing educational tools, webinars, seminars, workshops, and online courses.

2. Examination of the Market
Technical Analysis: To determine when to enter and exit an investment, use technical analysis tools and charting techniques to examine price patterns, trend lines, levels of support and resistance, volume indicators, and momentum oscillators.
To evaluate investment opportunities, perform fundamental analysis on businesses, sectors, and asset classes utilizing financial statements, earnings reports, cash flow analysis, valuation indicators, and comparative analysis.
Studying Economics: Keep an eye on economic data releases, macroeconomic indicators (such as GDP growth, inflation, interest, and unemployment rates), and policy effects to assess the state of the economy and market mood.

3. Due Diligence in Research Before Investing: Investigate possible investments thoroughly, taking into account competitive positioning, risk assessment, financial analysis, management appraisal, and company research.
Industry Trends: Keep abreast of how innovative technology, consumer tastes, legal changes, and developments in the global market affect investment possibilities and hazards.
Risk assessment: Determine which investment risks to be cautious of, such as currency risk, geopolitical risk, market risk, credit risk, liquidity risk, and operational risk. Then, adjust your risk management tactics accordingly.

4. Keep an eye on Portfolio Performance
Review on a regular basis: Evaluate the performance of each investment, asset allocation, sector exposures, returns, and risk-adjusted performance of the portfolio in relation to benchmarks and objectives.
As necessary, rebalance Periodically rebalance your portfolio to buy cheap assets, sell underperforming ones, realign asset allocations, and modify risk exposures in response to shifting market conditions and investing goals.

5. Modify Your Investment Approaches
Flexibility: Be flexible in your asset allocation and investing methods to accommodate changes in the market, economic cycles, geopolitical events, and unforeseen circumstances.
Adjustments for Tactics: Make tactical changes to your portfolio in response to sector rotations, short-term opportunities, market trends, valuation levels, and risk-return profiles.
Long-Term Vision: Maintain a long-term investment vision and strategic asset allocation in line with your financial objectives, time horizon, and risk tolerance, while balancing tactical short-term adjustments.

6. Employ Tools and Technology
Trading platforms, robo-advisors, investing platforms, and portfolio management technologies that provide real-time data, market insights, performance analytics, and risk assessment capabilities should all be used.

Automated Alerts: You can monitor investment positions, market movements, news updates, and changes in portfolio performance by setting up automated alerts, notifications, and price alerts.

7. Get Expert Counsel

Financial Advisors: Seek the counsel of licensed wealth managers, investment specialists, or financial advisors for individualized suggestions, portfolio evaluations, asset allocation plans, risk control techniques, and investment guidance.

Professional Networks: To share ideas, gain insights, and obtain a variety of viewpoints on investing possibilities and methods, get involved with professional networks, peer groups, industry associations, and investment clubs.

8. Examine and Take Note of Mistakes

Performance evaluation include post-trade analysis, performance evaluations, and investment reviews in order to pinpoint lessons learned, draw conclusions from successes and failures, and enhance decision-making procedures.

Adopt an attitude of continual improvement by reflecting on past mistakes, learning from them, responding to criticism, and fine-tuning investment strategy in light of actual results and market feedback.

In conclusion

Learning from experiences, market analysis, investment research, portfolio monitoring, tactical adjustments, harnessing technology, getting professional counsel, and staying educated are all necessary for staying on top of the game in the investing world. Through proactive, flexible, and knowledgeable behavior, investors can effectively navigate dynamic market conditions, maximize investment returns, and attain sustained financial prosperity.

Keep up with developments in the world economy, the stock market, and other areas that could affect your assets. Always keep learning, adjust your tactics, and think about getting help from financial experts when necessary.

Step 10: Evaluate and Correct

Your asset allocation will stay in line with your investing goals, risk tolerance, and market conditions if you routinely evaluate and rebalance your portfolio. To analyze and rebalance your portfolio, follow these essential steps:

1. Determine the Review Frequency
Periodic Reviews: Establish regular timeframes for portfolio reviews, such as quarterly, half-yearly, or yearly. Regular assessments enable you to monitor changes in the market and the performance of your portfolio.

2. Evaluation of Portfolio Performance
Compute the overall return of your investments, taking into account interest income, dividends, capital gains, and other investment returns. Evaluate your portfolio's performance in relation to pertinent benchmarks and objectives.
Risk-Adjusted Returns: To assess risk-adjusted returns, use measures such as the Sharpe ratio, which expresses performance as a function of volatility.

3. Consider Asset Distribution
Asset Class Allocation: Examine how much of each asset class—stocks, bonds, cash equivalents, real estate, and alternative investments—is allocated in your portfolio.
Goal Allocations: Based on your investing approach, risk tolerance, and long-term financial objectives, compare your present asset allocations to your desired proportions.

4. Adjust Asset Allocatives
Sell Overperforming Assets: If some investment categories or asset classes have fared much better than others, you might choose to sell some of them in order to reallocate funds to undervalued or underperforming assets.

Invest in underperforming assets that have room to grow or appreciate in value by allocating money from cash reserves or outperforming assets.

5. Tax Points to Take

Tax-Sensible Rebalancing When you rebalance your portfolio, take tax implications into consideration. Reduce tax liabilities by employing tax-efficient techniques such capital gains management, asset location optimization, and tax-loss harvesting.

6. Examine Each Investment

The performance of individual stocks, bonds, mutual funds, exchange-traded funds (ETFs), and other investment vehicles in your portfolio should be assessed.

Individual investments should be the subject of a fundamental study that takes into account various aspects like industry trends, competitive positioning, financial health, earnings growth, and valuation.

7. Take Market and Economic Trends Into Account

Examine macroeconomic patterns, economic indicators, changes in interest rates, inflation forecasts, and geopolitical events that could affect asset allocations and investing choices.

Market circumstances: To help you decide whether to rebalance your portfolio, keep an eye on market trends, sector rotations, volatility, investor sentiment, and market valuations.

8. Maintain Goal Alignment

Financial Objectives: Make sure that portfolio rebalancing is in line with your investment time horizon, risk tolerance, and liquidity requirements.

Changes in your Lifestyle: Take into account life events, shifts in your finances, retirement planning, financing for your children's education, and other aspects that can require modifying your investing plans.

9. Actions for Document Rebalancing

Confirmations of Trade: Hold records of all rebalancing activities for tracking and reporting needs, such as trade confirmations, transaction histories, tax paperwork, and investment statements.

Rebalancing Strategy: To inform future decisions, keep a record of your rebalancing strategy, target asset proportions, and rebalancing thresholds. You can also use this documentation to support portfolio modifications.

10. Look for Expert Counseling

See a Qualified Financial Advisor, Wealth Manager, or Investment Professional for Personalized Advice, Portfolio Analysis, Asset Allocation Strategies, and Rebalancing Recommendations.

In conclusion

To maintain the best possible asset allocation, control risk, and stay in line with your financial objectives, you must regularly examine and rebalance your investment portfolio. You may maximize investment returns and successfully navigate shifting market situations by analyzing portfolio performance, analyzing asset allocations, rebalancing as necessary, taking tax implications into account, keeping an eye on market trends, and consulting a professional.

When investing in stocks, one must first conduct thorough planning, study, research, and continuous observation. You may trade the stock market with confidence and work toward reaching your financial goals by adhering to these guidelines and maintaining a disciplined investing approach.

The Fundamentals of Investing: Creating Long-Term Value while Managing Risk

Investing is about building long-term value while skillfully managing risk, not just buying and selling shares. The following major pillars form the foundation of the ultimate investing principle:

1. Clearly defined objectives and budgeting

Establish Explicit Objectives: Whether your investment objectives are to save for retirement, finance college, buy a house, or become financially independent, start by outlining them precisely.
Budgeting: Make sure your goals, risk tolerance, investment horizon, liquidity requirements, and lifestyle aspirations are all reflected in a thorough financial plan.

2. Allocation of assets and diversification
Investing in a variety of asset types (stocks, bonds, cash equivalents, real estate, commodities) and geographical areas can help spread your risk and improve the resilience of your portfolio.
Asset Allocation: Choose an asset allocation plan that suits your risk tolerance, financial objectives, market circumstances, and prognosis for the economy. Periodically rebalance allocations to keep desired levels intact.

3. Investment Research and Fundamental Analysis
Essential Evaluation: Analyze prospective investments thoroughly from a fundamental standpoint, paying particular attention to the company's financial standing, increase in earnings, competitive advantages, market trends, and value measures.
Investment Research: Use ongoing data analysis, market insights, news updates, and research to stay up to date on industry dynamics, geopolitical events, economic changes, and market trends.

4. Extended-Term View

Patience and Discipline: Invest with a long-term outlook, prioritizing discipline, patience, and a focus on underlying value as opposed to cyclical market swings.

Compounding Returns: To increase the value of your investments over time, reinvest dividends, interest income, and capital gains to take advantage of compounding returns.

5. Risk Management and Capital Preservation Risk Assessment: Assess and manage investment risks, such as credit, market, liquidity, inflation, interest rate, currency, geopolitical, and regulatory concerns.

Preservation of Capital: Put capital preservation first by using asset allocation, diversification, risk management techniques, and wise investing choices.

6. Tax Management and Efficiency

Strategies That Save Taxes: To maximize after-tax returns, use tax-efficient investing methods, tax-deferred accounts, capital gains management, tax-loss harvesting, and retirement accounts (IRAs, 401(k)s).

Reduce investment costs as much as possible in order to improve net investment returns and long-term wealth building. These costs include expense ratios, management fees, transaction charges, and taxes.

7. Ongoing Education and Modification

Constant Learning: Make a commitment to learning new things constantly. Keep up with developments in technology, financial advances, regulations, and investment trends.

Adaptation: Continue to be flexible and adaptive in your approach to investing, modifying plans in response to shifting geopolitical situations, economic cycles, market conditions, and individual circumstances.

8. Expert Guidance and Cooperation

Financial Advisor Consultation: To formulate customized investment strategies, obtain portfolio analysis, and acquire access to specialized experience, think about consulting with certified financial advisors, wealth managers, or investment specialists.

Work together: To create comprehensive wealth management strategies that include investment planning, tax planning, estate planning, and risk management, work with investment specialists, legal consultants, tax advisers, and estate planners.

9. Responsible Investing and Ethical Issues

Moral Guidelines: Follow moral guidelines and responsible investing methods, taking into account social effect, sustainability standards, corporate governance procedures, and environmental, social, and governance (ESG) aspects while making investment decisions.

Impact Investing: Look into opportunities that support your values and contribute to positive social and environmental results through impact investing, socially responsible investing (SRI), sustainable investing, and ethical investing.

10. Go over, assess, and make changes

Continual Evaluations: Review and assess your financial objectives, asset allocations, risk exposures, performance measures, and investment portfolio on a regular basis.

Adjustments to the Portfolio: Adapt strategies, reallocate money, rebalance asset allocations, and make educated modifications to your portfolio in response to performance assessments, market analysis, and evolving investing goals.

In conclusion

Including goal clarity, diversification, fundamental analysis, risk management, long-term perspective, tax efficiency, ongoing learning, cooperation, ethical considerations, and adaptable methods, the ultimate concept of investing comprises a comprehensive approach to wealth management. Investors can pursue long-term value growth, financial stability, and wealth preservation while navigating challenging market conditions and accomplishing their financial objectives by adhering to these guidelines and tactics.

Jack Bogle stock market strategy

One of the pioneers of index investing and the creator of Vanguard Group, Jack Bogle, promoted a straightforward yet effective approach to stock market investing. The following are the main ideas behind Jack Bogle's stock market strategy:

1. Investing in exchange-traded funds (ETFs) or broad market index funds that track the performance of an entire market index, such the S&P 500 or the Total Stock Market Index, is known as index investing, and Bogle was a proponent of this strategy. Investing in the entire market allows investors to take advantage of overall market returns and achieve broad diversification.

2. Low-Cost Approach: Bogle highlighted the significance of reducing trading charges, expense ratios, and management fees when making investments. He promoted low-cost index funds or exchange-traded funds (ETFs) with competitive fees and charges because he thought that high costs eventually diminish investment profits.

3. Long-Term View: Bogle criticized frequent trading and market timing in favor of a long-term investing strategy. He thought that attempting to outperform the market by speculative or active trading is frequently ineffective and results in greater expenses and poorer profits.

4. Bogle emphasized the need for diversification in lowering investment risk. Investing in a diverse portfolio of index funds that encompass many asset classes such as stocks, bonds, and international markets can help investors spread their risk and lessen the impact of swings in specific stocks or sectors.

5. Stay the Course: Bogle promoted consistency and discipline in financial choices. He advised investors to maintain their investments despite market ups and downs, to keep detached from short-term emotional outbursts, and to concentrate on long-term financial objectives.

6. Dividend Reinvestment: In order to take advantage of compound growth over time, Bogle advised reinvesting dividends and capital gains from index funds. Reinvesting profits has the potential to greatly increase total returns on

investments, particularly when done in a way that is tax-efficient for retirement funds.

7. The philosophy of passive investing, which focuses on matching market returns rather than surpassing them, is the foundation of Bogle's investment strategy. In contrast to active management, he thought that steadily generating market returns over the long run—minus minimal fees—can produce better investment results.

8. Education and openness: Bogle was a fervent supporter of ethical business practices, openness, and investor education in the financial sector. He supported treating investors fairly, giving them access to information, and offering simple and uncomplicated investment options.

The main tenets of Jack Bogle's stock market approach are discipline, broad diversification, minimal costs, simplicity, and long-term orientation. His legacy of promoting passive index investing as a dependable and successful strategy for accumulating wealth and securing financial stability continues to have an impact on investors throughout the world.

Warren Buffett method of stock selection

Choosing companies in the same way as Warren Buffett requires a value investing strategy that emphasizes basic examination, long-term thinking, and responsible risk management. Here's a comprehensive guide on stock selection like Warren Buffett:

1. Recognize the fundamentals of value investing.

Intrinsic Value: Pay attention to determining a company's intrinsic value, which is a measure of its actual value derived from its fundamentals, including assets, cash flows, earnings, and growth potential.

Margin of Safety: To create a safety net that protects against losses and lowers investment risk, look for stocks that are trading below their true value.

2. Place a Focus on Fundamental Analysis

Financial Health: Determine a company's profitability, liquidity, solvency, and operational effectiveness by analyzing its financial statements, which include the income statement, balance sheet, and cash flow statement.

Analyze the quality of earnings, keeping an eye out for reliable and sustainable growth, robust cash flow production, and wise capital allocation.

Competitive Advantages: Determine which businesses have long-lasting advantages over their rivals, or economic moats, such as strong brands, high entry barriers, devoted clientele, and economies of scale.

3. Concentrate on Long-Term Outlooks

Business Quality: Put your money into companies that have solid management teams, a track record of success, distinct advantages over competitors, and room to grow over the long run.

Long-Term View: Set aside short-term speculation and concentrate on companies that have the potential to gradually multiply wealth. Adopt a long-term investment strategy.

4. Evaluation of Corporate Governance and Management

Management Quality: Assess the skill, moral character, and commitment of the organization's management to the interests of the shareholders. Seek for shareholder-friendly policies, sound capital allocation procedures, and open lines of communication.

Corporate Governance: Evaluate the company's adherence to best practices, executive remuneration structure, board independence, and corporate governance procedures.

5. Assessing Economic Moats

Examine and evaluate the origins of a business's competitive advantage, or economic moat. Think about things like intangible assets, switching costs, switching costs, network effects, and brand strength.

Invest in businesses that have long-term business sustainability, market share, and profit margin protection through sustainable competitive advantages.

6. Make Sense of the Businesses You Invest in

Circle of Competence: Make investments in sectors and companies that you are knowledgeable about. Steer clear of intricate ventures or sectors beyond your area of expertise.

Simple and Predictable: Give preference to companies whose income streams, business models, and industry dynamics are clear, simple, and predictable.

7. Search for Cheap Stocks

Valuation Metrics: To determine if a company is cheap in relation to its intrinsic worth, use valuation metrics like discounted cash flow (DCF) analysis and the price-to-earnings (P/E), price-to-book (P/B), and price-to-sales (P/S) ratios.

Contrarian Opportunities: Take into account contrarian opportunities, which arise when buying possibilities in fundamentally solid companies are created by market mispricing or brief setbacks.

8. Cautionary Risk Handling

Diversification: To lower company-specific risk and sector concentration, keep your portfolio diversified across several industries, sectors, and asset classes.

Margin of Safety: Invest with a margin of safety at all times to make sure that the stock's intrinsic value and the company's fundamentals will offset any potential negative risks.

9. Ongoing Education and Adjustment

Keep Up to Date: Keep an eye out for any changes in regulations, industry dynamics, market trends, or economic developments that might affect investing opportunities.

Adapt Strategies: Keep an open mind and be prepared to modify your investment plans in response to fresh data, shifting market dynamics, and evolving investing environments.

10. Self-control and patience

Long-Term Mentality: Retain a methodical and patient attitude when investing; stay away from speculating on the short term, timing the market, and making rash decisions.

Put Quality First: Put quality above quantity and concentrate on building a small but select portfolio of excellent companies with room to develop in the long run.

In summary:
Applying value investing principles, carrying out in-depth fundamental analysis, concentrating on long-term prospects, evaluating management caliber, spotting economic moats, investing in comprehensible companies, searching for undervalued opportunities, cautiously managing risk, ongoing education, and exercising patience and discipline when making investment decisions are all necessary when picking stocks like Warren Buffett. Investors might aim to create a profitable portfolio in line with Warren Buffett's value investing philosophy by adhering to these guidelines.

Peter Lynch Stock Market Strategy:

The renowned investor Peter Lynch, who formerly oversaw Fidelity Investments' Magellan Fund, is renowned for his effective stock market approach, which combines active stock selection with fundamental analysis. The following are the main tenets of Peter Lynch's stock market approach:

1. Invest in What You Know: Lynch recommended making investments in businesses and sectors that you are knowledgeable about and have experience with. He thought that individual investors had an advantage when they made investments in companies that they were familiar with, such as those that produced goods they used or were employed in.

2. lengthy-Term Investing: Lynch stressed how crucial it is to have a lengthy investment horizon. He urged investors to exercise patience and hold onto their money for long stretches of time in reputable businesses so that it has time to develop and compound.

3. Purchase Outstanding Companies: Lynch concentrated on finding outstanding companies with robust competitive advantages, sound financials, steady profits growth, and capable management teams. He sought out businesses that had resilient moats that shielded them from rivals.

4. Growth at a Reasonable Price (GARP): Lynch used an investment strategy called Growth at a Reasonable Price (GARP), which combined growth and value investing. He avoided pricey stocks in favor of businesses with solid growth potential and fair values.

5: Invest in Small and Mid-Cap firms: Lynch discovered chances in these firms that institutional investors had passed over. He thought these businesses offered greater potential for substantial returns and more space for expansion.
6. Lynch engaged in the technique of "scuttlebutt" investment, which entails obtaining information on businesses from a variety of sources, such as

suppliers, customers, workers, and industry experts. He was able to learn more about market trends and business operations thanks to this qualitative study.

7. Avoid Market Timing: Lynch cautioned against attempting to forecast short-term price changes or timing the market. He thought that timing the market was speculative and frequently resulted in lost chances and less than ideal profits.

8. Diversification Within Reason: Lynch supported both diversification within reason and concentrating on your greatest investment ideas. Having a diverse portfolio reduced susceptibility to individual stock movements and associated risk.

9. Be Contrarian and Patient: Lynch advised using contrarian behavior when needed and showing patience. He searched for opportunities in out-of-favor industries or equities, purchasing at a time when others were selling because of short-term losses or market pessimism.

10. Watch Your Investments: Lynch stressed the significance of keeping a close eye on investments and keeping up with company news, financial reports, market movements, and macroeconomic issues that may affect stock prices.

The main components of Peter Lynch's stock market approach were investing in reputable companies, carrying out in-depth research, maintaining an eye on long-term growth, exercising patience, and seizing chances in cheap or ignored equities. Many investors have been inspired by his methodical and systematic approach to stock selection, which is still relevant in the investing industry.

Benjamin Graham Stock Market Strategy

Benjamin Graham, who is frequently called the "Father of Value Investing," created a systematic, fundamentally-based approach to the stock market that has impacted numerous generations of investors. Benjamin Graham's stock market strategy is based on the following fundamental ideas:

1. Value Investing: The ideas of value investing, which center on finding cheap stocks that are selling below their true worth, served as the foundation for Graham's methodical approach to investing. In his opinion, the market frequently overvalues or undervalues equities in the near run, giving patient investors opportunities.

2. Margin of Safety: Graham considered the idea of the margin of safety to be one of his core ideas. In order to guard against downside risk, he stressed buying equities with a wide margin of safety, which means the stock's price should be well below its intrinsic value.

3. Graham was a strong supporter of in-depth fundamental examination of stocks, with an emphasis on quantitative elements like earnings, book value, cash flow, debt levels, dividend history, and future growth potential. In order to find cheap stocks, he created methods such as the Graham Number and the Net Current Asset Value (NCAV).

4. Graham had a conservative investment philosophies that put capital preservation and risk minimization first. He cautioned against market timing, speculative investing, and placing too much focus on short-term price fluctuations.

5. Viewpoint Over Time: Graham was a proponent of long-term investing rather than speculating in the near term. He advised investors to exercise patience and hold high-quality equities through periods of market volatility in order to give fundamental value time to materialize.

6. Graham espoused the benefits of diversity in lowering risk and preventing overexposure to certain equities or industry sectors. To attain a well-balanced portfolio, he suggested distributing investments among several businesses and asset classes.

7. Graham used a contrarian approach, searching for chances in stocks or industries that were out of style. Astute investors could find undervalued possibilities due to market inefficiencies and emotional biases, according to him.

8. Emotional Self-Control: Graham placed a strong emphasis on emotional self-control and sound investing judgment. He counseled avoiding panic or market excitement in favor of careful research and methodical investing techniques.

9. Investment Margin: Graham advised choosing stocks and managing a portfolio while keeping a margin of safety. He recommended holding a cash reserve or allocating a segment of the portfolio to more secure investments in order to manage market volatility.

10. Constant Learning: Graham emphasized the significance of keeping abreast of changes in the financial markets, the economy, investment strategies, and financial analytical methods. He thought that knowledgeable investors were capable of making wiser choices.

The main tenets of Benjamin Graham's stock market strategy include diversification, contrarian thinking, long-term perspective, margin of safety, value investing, fundamental analysis, conservative principles, emotional control, and ongoing learning. His timeless lessons have helped investors reduce risk, find inherent value, and make profitable long-term investments.

Gaining profits via Exchange-Traded Funds (ETFs):

Exchange-traded funds, or ETFs, can be profitable if one knows their features, chooses the best ETFs, and puts winning methods into practice. This is a thorough guide that explains how to profit from ETFs:

Learn the Fundamentals of ETFs
Investment funds known as exchange-traded funds (ETFs) are traded on stock exchanges and provide exposure to a diverse portfolio of assets, including stocks, bonds, commodities, and real estate.
Liquidity: Because ETFs can be bought or sold at market prices at any time during the trading day, they offer liquidity.
diversity: ETFs reduce sector or individual stock risk by investing in a portfolio of securities. This provides the benefits of diversity.

2. Choose the Correct ETFs
Asset Class: Select exchange-traded funds (ETFs) based on your investing objectives and risk tolerance. You can choose ETFs related to stocks, fixed income, commodities, currencies, or alternative assets.
Active ETFs versus Index: Select actively managed ETFs, which seek to beat the market, or index-tracking ETFs, which follow a benchmark index.
ETFs with low expense ratios are a good choice if you want to cut costs and increase returns.

3. Techniques for Investing
Prolonged Investing: Use an ETF buy-and-hold strategy to benefit from compound returns and asset appreciation as you build long-term wealth.
Sector Rotation: Invest in sector-specific ETFs in accordance with industry trends, economic cycles, and sector performance expectations to put sector rotation techniques into practice.
Income Generation: Choose bonds or dividend-focused exchange-traded funds (ETFs) to receive regular payments of interest or dividends.

4. Managing Risk and Diversification

Asset Allocation: To reduce risk and maximize returns, use exchange-traded funds (ETFs) to diversify across countries and asset classes, such as equities, bonds, real estate, and commodities.

Risk-Adjusted Returns: If you're looking for ETFs that focus on achieving consistent performance in relation to volatility, take a look at them.

5. Circumstances and the Market

Market Timing: Based on economic indicators, technical analysis, and market sentiment, use exchange-traded funds (ETFs) for tactical asset allocation and market timing.

Market circumstances: ETF holdings should be adjusted in response to changes in interest rates, inflation forecasts, geopolitical events, economic outlooks, and market conditions.

6. Efficiency in Taxes

Invest in ETFs through tax-advantaged accounts, such as Individual Retirement Accounts (IRAs) or 401(k) plans, to take advantage of tax deferrals and tax-free gains.

Employ tax-loss harvesting techniques using exchange-traded funds (ETFs) to offset capital gains and lower your taxable income.

7. Put Dividends and Distributions Back into Account

Dividend Reinvestment: To benefit from compound interest and accelerate long-term wealth creation, reinvest dividends and distributions from exchange-traded funds (ETFs).

DRIP Plans: To have dividends automatically reinvested into more shares, sign up for a Dividend Reinvestment Plan (DRIP), which is provided by ETF providers.

8. Frequent Checking and Adjusting

Portfolio Review: To evaluate portfolio performance and make wise decisions, keep a close eye on ETF holdings, performance measures, asset allocation, and market movements.

Rebalancing: Adjust exposure in response to shifting market conditions and rebalance ETF holdings on a regular basis to maintain target asset allocation percentages.

9. Prevent Making Emotional Choices

Remain Disciplined: Remain detached from the short-term market noise and swings, focus on long-term objectives, and exercise discipline in your investment approach to prevent emotional decision-making.

Ignore the noise in the market: Pay attention to basic analysis, investing research, and strategic asset allocation; ignore daily market movements and news headlines.

10. Become Informed and Seek Expert Counsel

Constant Learning: Keep up with industry news, research, and education to keep informed about ETFs, investment strategies, market trends, and financial planning principles.

Seeking Expert Advice: For individualized counsel, portfolio evaluation, risk assessment, and investment suggestions, think about speaking with a financial advisor or other qualified financial specialist.

In conclusion:

Investing in ETFs requires disciplined investing, tax efficiency, reinvestment of dividends, diversification, smart asset allocation, risk management, and market trend knowledge. You can take advantage of the advantages of exchange-traded funds (ETFs) to grow wealth, accomplish financial objectives, and manage different market circumstances by choosing the appropriate ETFs, putting good investment methods into practice, and practicing discipline.

Dividend stocks: A Way to Generate Passive Income

Building a portfolio of dividend-paying companies that consistently produce cash flow through dividends is the first step in using dividend stocks to create passive income. This comprehensive guide explains how to use dividend stocks to generate passive income:

Gain a Basic Understanding of Dividend Investing
Dividends: As a distribution of profits, firms pay dividends to their shareholders in the form of cash.
Dividend Return: The annual dividend amount per share divided by the stock price, given as a percentage, is the dividend yield.
Companies having a track record of steadily raising dividends over a long period of time are known as dividend aristocrats.

2. Picking Equities with Dividends
Dividend History: As a sign of a company's strength and dedication to its shareholders, look for companies that have a history of consistent or rising dividends throughout time.
Dividend Yield: Examine equities with appealing dividend yields in comparison to industry averages and peers, but also evaluate the yield's sustainability.
Dividend Growth: Companies with a track record of increasing dividends should be given priority as they can eventually boost passive income and serve as a hedge against inflation.

3. Diversify Your Portfolio: To lower risk and exposure to issues unique to a certain industry, invest in dividend stocks from a variety of industries.
Size of Company: To balance risk and possible rewards, think about diversifying across dividend-paying large-cap, mid-cap, and small-cap firms.
Discover dividend-paying equities from several geographical areas to spread your currency risk and profit from the expansion of the world economy.
4. Reinvest Profits

DRIPs, or dividend reinvestment plans, are: To compound your returns, sign up for company-sponsored dividend reinvestment plans (DRIPs) or use brokerage services that offer ADR.
Compound Growth: Reinvesting dividends can result in long-term compound growth that will raise your passive income and wealth accumulation considerably.

5. Assess Sustainability of Dividends
Dividend Payout Ratio: Use this metric to determine whether a firm can continue paying dividends without jeopardizing its financial stability. It is calculated by dividing total dividends paid by earnings.
Analyze a company's free cash flow to make sure it has enough cash on hand to pay dividends, fund operations, and finance expansion plans.

6. Long-Term Investing Approach: Be Patient: When it comes to dividend stocks, have a long-term investing approach. It takes time and patience to create a significant passive income stream.
Dividend Reinvestment: Over time, reinvest dividends to take advantage of compound interest and optimize the potential for passive income.

7. Take a look at dividend funds and ETFs.
Examine mutual funds and exchange-traded funds (ETFs) that are specifically focused on dividends. They provide diverse exposure to a portfolio of dividend-paying stocks from a range of industries and geographical areas.
Take into consideration dividend growth funds, which make investments in businesses that have a track record of raising dividends and offer the possibility for both income and growth.

8. Risk Control
Diversification: To lower the risk associated with particular equities and sector concentration, keep a diverse portfolio of dividend-paying companies.
High-quality companies should be your main focus. They should have sound balance sheets, enduring business plans, distinct advantages over competitors, and a proven dividend history.

9. Tax-related Matters

Accounts that are Tax-Efficient: To take advantage of tax-deferred or tax-free growth, invest in dividend stocks through tax-advantaged accounts like Individual Retirement Accounts (IRAs) or 401(k) plans.

Dividends that Qualify: Recognize how dividends are treated tax-wise, since qualifying dividends may be taxed at a lower rate for qualified investors than regular income.

10. Be Educated and Flexible

Never-ending Education: Keep yourself updated on market movements, financial news, and business changes that could affect passive income techniques and dividend stocks.

Adjustment: When it comes to investing, be flexible and willing to make adjustments to portfolio allocations in response to shifting market conditions, economic cycles, and investment possibilities.

In conclusion

Investing in dividend stocks to generate passive income requires choosing high-quality dividend-paying companies, diversifying your holdings, reinvesting dividends for compound growth, keeping an eye on dividend sustainability, taking a long-term approach to investing, taking dividend-focused funds or exchange-traded funds into consideration, managing risk, maximizing tax efficiency, remaining informed, and responding to market conditions. Investors can gradually create a steady and expanding passive income stream by implementing these techniques.

PIEs and Value Investing:

In investment research and portfolio management, value investing and PIE (Price-to-Earnings-to-Growth) ratios are fundamental ideas. Here is a further explanation of each subject:

Worth Investing

A technique for investing in equities that are undervalued and trading below their intrinsic worth is called value investing. Value investing's basic tenet is to purchase equities at a discount to their actual value with the goal of long-term capital growth while controlling risk. A few important facets of value investing are:

Intrinsic worth: Value investors examine core elements such profits, cash flows, assets, liabilities, growth potential, and industry position in order to determine a company's intrinsic worth.

Margin of Safety: In order to reduce the risk of a downturn and increase possible returns, value investors look to purchase stocks at a substantial discount to their true value.
Investing in out-of-favor or ignored stocks that the market undervalues because of transient setbacks, market sentiment, or immediate difficulties is a contrarian technique that value investors frequently use.

worth Investing: Value investing prioritizes a long-term investment perspective, concentrating on the intrinsic worth of companies instead of speculative or short-term market movements.

Growth-to-Earnings-to-Price, or PIE, In ratios

A valuation indicator used to evaluate a stock's valuation in relation to its earnings growth rate is the PIE ratio, sometimes referred to as the PEG ratio. The Price-to-Earnings (P/E) ratio is combined with the earnings growth rate of the company to determine if a stock is overpriced or undervalued in relation to its potential for future growth. To find the PIE ratio, use the following formula:

The PIE Ratio

=

P/E Ratio

Rate of Earnings Growth

PIE Coefficient:

Rate of Earnings Growth

P/E Ratio

Here is more information about PIE ratios and their importance:

Interpretation: A stock may be undervalued in relation to its potential for profits growth if the PIE ratio is less than 1. In light of its growth pace, a ratio greater than one can indicate that a company is overpriced.

Earnings Growth: In addition to taking into account the present earnings multiple (P/E ratio), the PIE ratio also takes the company's earnings growth rate into account. In comparison to peers, a lower PIE ratio could suggest a more appealing valuation.

Growth Prospects: The PIE ratio is used by investors to determine if the price of a stock is reasonable given the anticipated rate of earnings growth. An opportunity for investment may be indicated by a low PIE ratio in comparison to a strong rate of profits growth.

Limitations: A company's fundamentals, risks, and potential for future growth may not be fully captured by the PIE ratio. Along with qualitative analysis and additional valuation indicators, it should be used.

To sum up, value investing is the process of purchasing cheap stocks using a long-term outlook and fundamental examination. A valuation metric called the PIE ratio compares a stock's valuation to its growth prospects by taking into account both the P/E ratio and the earnings growth rate. When evaluating investment prospects and reaching well-informed conclusions, investors can benefit greatly from both ideas.

Would you like to learn more about PIE ratios, value investing in particular, or other related subjects?

Investing in Growth Stocks to Gain Profit:

Long-term wealth generation through growth stock investing can be highly profitable. Shares of businesses predicted to develop faster than usual in relation to the overall market or their industry peers are known as growth stocks. This is an explanation of how to profit from growth stocks:

Comprehend Growth Investing
Investments in growth firms are those that have the potential for significant earnings growth, creative business strategies, a competitive edge, and market leadership positions.
Risk and Return: Growth stocks can lead to large wealth development and capital appreciation, but they also carry a higher degree of volatility and risk.

2. Find Areas for Growth
Market Trends: Determine the new and developing trends, disruptive technology, shifting consumer tastes, and industry dynamics that propel the expansion of particular industries.
Evaluation of the Company: To assess growth measures like profit margins, market share expansion, earnings growth rates, revenue growth rates, and return on equity (ROE), perform fundamental analysis.

3. Choosing Progression Stocks
High-quality businesses: Search for reputable businesses that have the potential for steady growth, capable management teams, cutting-edge goods and services, and a competitive edge.
Sound Financial Position: Examine the growth firms' financials in terms of their cash flow, debt levels, liquidity positions, and strength of their balance sheets.

4. Investment Horizon for the Long Run

Patience: Growth stocks may take longer to show meaningful growth, so have a long-term investment perspective. Keep your attention on the company's core growth drivers and steer clear of speculative thinking.
Reinvesting dividends or capital gains might help to maximize wealth building over time by compounding returns.

5. Track Metrics of Growth
Quarterly Profit: To evaluate the success of the company in comparison to expectations, track patterns in earnings growth and quarterly earnings reports.
Revenue increase: Monitor rates of increase for revenue, trends in customer acquisition, tactics for market expansion, and advancements in the sales pipeline.

6. Control Risk Diversification: To lower the risk associated with sector concentration and company-specific risk, diversify your portfolio among several growth stocks and industries.
Risk assessment: Consider and control the risks related to growth investing, such as macroeconomic variables, market, industry, and competitive risks as well as regulatory concerns.

7. Taking Value Into Account
Evaluation Measures: To determine whether a growth stock is appropriately valued or overvalued, apply valuation criteria such as discounted cash flow (DCF) analysis, price-to-earnings (P/E), price-to-sales (P/S), and price-to-book (P/B) measurements.
Growth Premium: You may be able to pay more for high-growth companies, but you should make sure that the company's earnings potential and growth prospects support the value.

8. Remain Vigilant and Adjust Research: Remain vigilant regarding market patterns, sector breakthroughs, technology breakthroughs, legislative modifications, and competitive terrain transitions.
Adaptation: Be open to changing your investing methods in response to fresh data, shifting market dynamics, and evolving growth prospects.

9. Review and Rebalance Your Portfolio: Regularly review and rebalance your portfolio to incorporate fresh growth prospects, cut outperforming stocks, and realign asset allocations.
Conduct monthly performance reviews of your growth stocks, compare them to peers or pertinent indices, and determine risk-adjusted returns.

10. Consult a Professional
Consultation with a certified Financial Advisor: For individualized guidance, portfolio analysis, risk evaluation, and growth stock suggestions, think about scheduling a consultation with a certified financial advisor or investment expert.

In conclusion
Finding high-growth opportunities, picking reputable businesses with promising growth prospects, establishing a long-term investment horizon, keeping an eye on growth metrics, controlling risk, evaluating valuations, remaining informed, adjusting strategies, rebalancing portfolios, and getting expert assistance when necessary are all necessary to profit from growth stocks. Investors that implement these techniques have the ability to accumulate large wealth over time and take advantage of growth opportunities.

Using initial public offerings (IPOs) to generate revenue

Gaining financial success from initial public offerings (IPOs) requires a thorough understanding of the IPO procedure, opportunity evaluation, risk management, and strategic investing methods. IPO profit-making tips are provided here:

1. Be familiar with the IPO Process

A private firm offers its shares to the public for the first time through an initial public offering (IPO), which enables investors to purchase shares and take a stake in the business.
Investment banks assist in underwriting initial public offerings (IPOs) by helping to price the shares, publicize the offering, and ease the transfer of ownership from private to public.

2. Assess Prospects for an IPO
Analyze the company in-depth, taking into account its business plan, competitive advantages, industry standing, financial results, potential for expansion, management group, and potential risks.
Examine the prospectus carefully, as it contains comprehensive details on the business's finances, activities, risks, use of proceeds, and IPO pricing.

3. Think About Investment Requirements
High-quality businesses: IPOs of reputable businesses with solid foundations, room to grow sustainably, cutting-edge goods and services, and competitive advantages should be the main focus.
Examine the IPO's valuation in light of its competitors, industry standards, growth rates, earnings potential, and long-term prospects.
Assess and handle the risks involved in investing in initial public offerings (IPOs). These risks include those related to the market, industry,

company-specific factors, regulations, competitive environments, and lock-up periods.
Portfolio diversification can help lower risk exposure and prevent overconcentration in initial public offering (IPO) investments.

Engage in first public offerings
Direct Participation: You may be able to buy shares directly from the initial public offering (IPO) by using brokerage accounts that grant access to primary market offers.
Allocation Size: Based on your investment objectives, overall investment strategy, portfolio diversification, and risk tolerance, decide how much to invest in an initial public offering (IPO).

6. Approaches to Strategic Investment
Trading IPO Shares Short-Term: Some investors may trade IPO shares short-term in an effort to profit on early price swings, market sentiment, and trading volume.
Adopt a long-term investing strategy when it comes to initial public offerings (IPOs), concentrating on businesses that have the potential for rapid growth, distinct advantages over competitors, and viable business plans.

7. Remain Educated and Track Effectiveness of Market Research: Keep up with news on impending initial public offerings (IPOs), industry advancements, market trends, economic indicators, and legislative changes that could affect IPO investments.
Performance tracking: Keep tabs on corporate advancements, earnings reports, quarterly results, industry trends, and IPO investment performance to evaluate investment success and make wise choices.

8. Get Expert Counsel
Seeking Advice from a skilled Financial Advisor or Investment expert: For individualized guidance, risk evaluation, allocation plans, and investment suggestions, think about seeking advice from a skilled financial advisor or investment expert.

9. Comprehend Lock-Up Times
Lock-Up Period: After an IPO, insiders, staff members, and initial investors are prohibited from selling their shares. Be mindful at these times. Keep an eye on lock-up expirations since they could affect share values.

10. Examine the Post-IPO Trading Market Reaction: Evaluate the market's responses to initial public offerings (IPOs), taking into account changes in price, trading volume, investor sentiment, analyst coverage, and institutional investor involvement.
Trading Strategies: Depending on the state of the market and the performance of initial public offerings, take into account various trading strategies including growth investment, value investing, momentum trading, or contrarian approaches.

In conclusion
Profiting from initial public offerings (IPOs) requires assessing prospects, carrying out in-depth analysis, controlling risks, using strategic investment methods, keeping track of results, remaining educated, and, if necessary, obtaining expert counsel. Investors may be able to take advantage of IPO chances and make money by comprehending the IPO process, evaluating investment criteria, engaging strategically, controlling risk, and keeping up with market developments.

Opportunities and Market Capitalization

One important indicator of the size and worth of a publicly listed firm is market capitalization, sometimes known as market cap. The computation involves multiplying the current share price of the corporation by the total number of outstanding shares. Market capitalization offers information about a company's size, growth potential, risk profile, and investment appeal, making it a crucial consideration when assessing investment prospects. Below is a summary of market capitalization and the investment options it offers:

Market Capitalization Types:

1. Big-Cap stocks: These are businesses that are usually valued at more than $10 billion on the market. These businesses frequently have a long history, are well-known in the industry, and could provide dividend income and stability.
Stocks in the mid-cap category: These stocks are valued between $2 billion and $10 billion on the market. They frequently have the ability to grow at a reasonable rate, strike a balance between stability and growth, and occasionally present chances for financial gains.
Market capitalizations of small-cap stocks are typically less than $2 billion. They provide better growth potential but also higher volatility and risk because they are usually younger businesses or those in developing industries.

2. Opportunities for Investments Based on Market Capitalization
Opportunities for Large-Caps: Stability, dividend income, and exposure to reputable, internationally operating corporations are all benefits that large-cap stocks can offer. Large-cap stocks with robust financial performance, steady profits growth, and strong competitive advantages may present chances to investors.
Mid-Cap Prospects: The risk and growth potential of mid-cap equities are well-balanced. These businesses could be growing their market share, operating in sectors of the economy that are seeing growth, or using creative

business methods. Mid-cap stocks may be beneficial to investors looking for growth prospects at a moderate risk level.
chances with Large Growth Potential: Small-cap companies offer chances with large growth potential, but they also carry a higher risk and volatility. Small-cap stocks may be of interest to investors pursuing aggressive growth strategies, especially those with disruptive technology, niche markets, or cutting-edge goods and services.

3. Risk vs. Growth Potential Aspects
Potential for Growth: One measure of potential for growth is market capitalization. Because they are smaller, more flexible, and have more capacity for growth than large-cap equities, small- and mid-cap stocks frequently have better growth potential.
Risk considerations: Although larger corporations (large-cap stocks) may expand more slowly, they may also offer more stability and reduced volatility. On the other hand, smaller businesses (small-cap and mid-cap stocks) could be more volatile in terms of price, but they also present chances for quick capital growth.

Section and Industry Concentration
Allocation by Sector: Market capitalization factors may also be used within particular sectors or industries. For instance, investors in technology businesses may find possibilities in tech stocks with innovative products or services, whether they are mid-cap or small-cap.
Sector Trends: To find investment possibilities across various market capitalization segments, analyze industry trends and development potential. While small-cap or mid-cap stocks may present superior investing opportunities, certain industries might be better suited for large-cap investments.

5. Methods of Diversification
The process of diversifying a portfolio involves taking market capitalization into account. To achieve a balance between prospective returns and risk, a

well-diversified portfolio may contain a combination of large-, mid-, and small-cap equities.

Risk management: Reducing exposure to any one firm, industry, or market segment can be achieved by diversifying among market capitalization segments. It enables investors to seize opportunities at various stages of an economy's cycle and a company's growth.

6. Metrics for Evaluation

Evaluation Measures: Take valuation indicators like Price-to-Earnings (P/E), Price-to-Book (P/B), Price-to-Sales (P/S), and earnings growth rates into account when assessing investment opportunities based on market capitalization. When evaluating the relative attractiveness of equities within each market cap group, these criteria can be useful.

In conclusion

When assessing investment prospects across a range of firm sizes, growth potentials, risk profiles, and sectors/industries, market capitalization offers a framework. Based on market capitalization factors, investors may customize their investment plans to balance diversification, risk management, and growth potential. Investors can make well-informed selections that are in line with their investing objectives, risk tolerance, and portfolio diversification goals by being aware of the traits and opportunities associated with large-cap, mid-cap, and small-cap stocks.

Ten costly Mistakes Beginners Make:

1. Lack of Clear Financial Goals: This error occurs when there is a lack of clarity on financial objectives, such as saving for a significant purchase, planning for retirement, or accumulating wealth.

• Impact: A lack of direction can result in impulsive investing choices, mismatched risk tolerance, and the inability to monitor financial goals.

• Remedy: Establish clear financial objectives with deadlines, budgets, and risk tolerance levels. Make sure your investing techniques are in line with these objectives to guarantee a methodical and deliberate approach.

2. Ignoring due diligence and research

• Error: Purchasing securities or assets without fully investigating the market, comprehending the underlying principles, and evaluating the dangers.

• Impact: Enhanced vulnerability to underperforming assets, volatile markets, and unanticipated losses.

• Recommendation: Give study and due diligence top priority before making any financial decisions. To make wise investment decisions, examine firm financials, market dynamics, industry trends, and economic aspects.

3. Only Paying Attention to High Returns

Making the mistake of chasing large returns without taking volatility, risk, and investment suitability into account.

• Impact: Giving in to investment fraud, speculative plans, or high-risk ventures that make big promises but frequently end up with huge losses.

• Approach to investment should be balanced, taking long-term growth potential, diversity, and risk-adjusted returns into account. Refrain from making investments that seem too good to be true or that offer inflated profits.

4. Not Increasing Investment Variety

• Error: Not diversifying over a range of investments and instead concentrating assets in a particular industry, firm, or asset class.

• Impact: A concentrated portfolio is more vulnerable to market downturns, exposure to risks unique to a certain industry, and a lack of diversification.

The answer is to diversify your investments across industries, geographies, asset classes (stocks, bonds, and real estate), and investment strategies in order to minimize risk and maximize profits.

5. Ignoring Your Emergency Money

• Error: Forgetting to put emergency money away for unforeseen costs, crises, or brief financial difficulties.

• Effect: Investments were forced to be liquidated at disadvantageous times, resulting in penalties, taxes, and possible losses to pay for unforeseen costs.

The answer is to create an emergency fund that is large enough to cover three to six months' worth of living expenses and keep it in a liquid, easily accessible account before making investments in more hazardous securities.

6. Overtrading and Timing of Markets

• Error: Buying and selling investments frequently depending on transient market fluctuations in an effort to timing the market for rapid gains.

• Impact: Higher taxes, transaction expenses, and possible losses from ill-timed trades, volatile markets, and emotional decision-making.

- Suggestion: Steer clear of excessive trading, concentrate on strategic asset allocation, and adopt a long-term investing strategy. Remain disciplined, disregard gyrations in the market, and adhere to your investment strategy.

7. Ignoring the Effects of Taxes

- Error: Not taking into account tax implications, dividends, capital gains, and tax-effective investing techniques.

- Effects include increased tax obligations, lost chances to optimize taxes, and lower investment after-tax returns.

- Solution: Use tax-advantaged accounts (401(k)s and IRAs, for example), tax-loss harvesting techniques, and tax professionals for advice. Also, educate yourself on the tax ramifications of various assets.

8. Managing Emotions in the Face of Market Volatility

- Error: During times of market turbulence, letting feelings like fear, greed, or panic dictate financial choices.

- Impact: Departing from long-term investment objectives, selling investments at a loss, and making irrational decisions can all have an impact.

- Resolved: Steer clear of emotionally driven snap decisions, stick to a disciplined investment strategy, ignore short-term market noise, and concentrate on long-term objectives.

9. Not Often Rebalancing the Portfolio

- Error: Not rebalancing investment portfolios on a regular basis to realign investment objectives, risk tolerance, and asset allocations.

• Impact: Missed chances to maximize portfolio performance, excessive exposure to particular asset classes, and departure from desired risk profiles.

• Solution: Put into practice a methodical rebalancing plan, evaluate portfolio allocations on a regular basis (such as annually or semi-annually), and make investment adjustments to preserve the appropriate levels of risk and asset allocation.

10. A lack of self-control and patience

• Error: Not adhering to long-term investing strategies, expecting quick results, and becoming disheartened by transient market swings.

• Impact: Losing out on possibilities for long-term investments, compound growth, and the strength of maintaining investments through market cycles.

• Remedy: When it comes to investing, develop patience, self-control, and a long-term outlook. Maintain your investing strategy, give fundamental analysis your full attention, and refrain from responding hastily to transient market fluctuations.

Novice investors can enhance their investing results, lay a strong basis for future success, and effectively pursue their financial objectives by steering clear of these frequent pitfalls.

IDEAL TIMING FOR STOCK BUYING:

Accurately timing the stock market is difficult and frequently unattainable since investor emotions, economic conditions, and market swings can all change significantly. Still, there are a number of guidelines and tactics that investors should take into account while searching for favorable moments to purchase stocks:

1. Long-Term Investment Horizon: Rather than attempting to time transient market fluctuations, concentrate on long-term investing. Investors that remain committed over the long term and ride out market cycles have historically made good returns.

2. Value Investing: Search for cheap stocks with sound fundamentals, including low Price-to-profits (P/E) ratios, high profits growth prospects, sound balance sheets, and an edge over competitors in their respective markets.

3. Market Dips or Corrections: Invest in equities when there are downturns, corrections, or spikes in volatility in the market. Discounted prices on high-quality stocks can be obtained during market pullbacks.

4. Dollar-Cost Averaging: Use this technique to invest a set amount of money into the market on a regular basis, irrespective of brief price swings. Over time, this strategy may help reduce average purchase prices and lessen the effects of market volatility.

5. Buy on Fear, Sell on Greed: Warren Buffett's well-known maxim advises purchasing when the market is scared (a time of market pessimism) and selling when the market is greedy (a time of market exuberance). Going against the grain and taking advantage of extremes in market sentiment is known as contrarian investing.

6. Company Earnings and outlook: Keep an eye on quarterly results, company earnings reports, and outlook revisions. Stock price increases might be sparked by high growth forecasts or positive profit surprises.

7. Industry and Sector Trends: Determine whether businesses or sectors have long-term investment potential due to demographic changes, technological breakthroughs, positive growth prospects, or favorable regulatory tailwinds.

Dividend equities should be taken into consideration. These stocks should have sustainable cash flows, good dividend coverage ratios, and continuous dividend increases. Dividend equities offer prospective capital growth along with income streams.

9. technical analysis: To find possible entry points, support levels, and resistance levels, use chart patterns and technical analysis tools. For a more thorough approach to investing, however, combine technical and fundamental analysis.

10. Risk Management: Make wise decisions about your portfolio's diversification, reasonable goal-setting, evaluation of your risk tolerance, and avoid concentrated bets on a few select stocks or excessive leverage.

Although there might not be a "perfect" moment to purchase stocks, investors can make educated selections and successfully manage the challenges of stock market investing by concentrating on fundamental analysis, long-term investment strategies, disciplined investing principles, and keeping up with market movements. Making investing selections requires careful consideration of personal financial situations, extensive study, and advice from financial counselors or other experts in the field.

WHEN TO SALE A STOCK:

One of the most important aspects of investment management is determining when to sell a stock, which involves carefully weighing a number of criteria. Here are some crucial circumstances in which it might be appropriate to sell stock:

1. Achieving Investment Goals: It can be appropriate to sell the stock if it has grown to your target price or produced the anticipated returns needed to attain your financial goals.

2. Fundamental Shifts: Offload the company in the event that there are noteworthy adverse shifts in its core competencies, including diminishing earnings, reduced profit margins, managerial concerns, or a deterioration in the company's competitive standing.

3. Overvaluation: It would be wise to sell the stock and make a profit if key indicators such as the Price-to-Earnings (P/E), Price-to-Book (P/B), or Price-to-Sales (P/S) ratios indicate that the stock has become overvalued.

4. Diversification Requirements: Selling some shares might help rebalance and lower risk exposure if your portfolio becomes unduly concentrated in a certain stock or industry.

5. Loss Limitation: Reduce losses if the stock continuously performs below your risk threshold, if the initial investment premise is no longer valid, or both.

6. Market Conditions: If there is a chance that the stock's performance and future prospects will be badly impacted by market downturns, economic uncertainty, or geopolitical events, you should think about selling.

7. Dividend Changes: A reassessment of the investment may be necessary if a dividend-paying stock suspends or cuts its dividends. This could be a sign of underlying financial difficulties.

8. Tax Considerations: Before selling, assess the tax implications, taking into account things like long-term versus short-term capital gains, opportunities to harvest tax losses, and overall tax strategy.

9. Rebalancing: To preserve desired asset allocations, risk tolerances, and investing goals, periodically examine and rebalance your portfolio. This may entail selling some equities.

10. Opportunity Cost: Sell if you find better places to invest where the possibility of earning larger returns justifies parting with the present stock.

It's critical to base your choice to sell a stock on a variety of factors, including market conditions, tax implications, risk management guidelines, financial objectives, and fundamental analysis. Steer clear of rash or emotional selections, and check your portfolio frequently to be sure it fits in with your overall financial plan. Furthermore, seeking advice from a financial counselor or investment specialist can offer insightful information and direction for making wise selling selections.

THE SECRET METHODS TO MAKE MONEY FROM UNPROGRESSIVE STOCK

Making money on a stock that is sideways moving or stagnant—that is, not seeing large price fluctuations—can be difficult, but it is not impossible. The following are some tactics and things to think about in order to possibly profit from these stocks:

1. Recognize the Causes of Stability

Fundamental Analysis: Evaluate the company's competitive position, growth prospects, industry dynamics, business model, and financials in detail. Determine the reasons behind the stock's inaction, such as consistent profitability, market saturation, difficulties with regulations, or problems unique to the industry.

2. Assess market sentiment and valuation

Valuation indicators: Use basic indicators such as price-to-earnings (P/E), price-to-book (P/B), price-to-sales (P/S), and earnings growth potential to evaluate the stock's valuation. Ascertain whether the stock, in relation to its competitors and industry benchmarks, is properly valued, undervalued, or overvalued.

Market Sentiment: Keep an eye on news developments pertaining to the firm or industry, analyst recommendations, institutional investment activity, and market sentiment. Stock prices can be impacted by positive sentiment swings.

3. Strategies for Income Generation

Investing in dividends: Take into account dividend-paying companies that have high dividend coverage ratios, steady dividend growth, and appealing dividend yields. Even in the case of a stagnant stock price, dividend income can still generate a consistent flow of revenue.

Covered Calls: Use techniques for covered call options to profit from equities that are stationary. Sell call options in opposition to your current stock holdings to earn premiums and maybe profit if the stock stays unchanged or makes small increases.

4. Trading strategies and technical analysis

Finding price ranges or support/resistance levels where the stock has been moving sideways is known as range-bound trading. To profit from short-term price changes, use range-bound trading methods such as buying near support levels and selling near resistance levels.

Volatility Trading: Even in a sideways market, you can profit from possible price fluctuations or heightened volatility by using volatility-based trading tactics like straddles and strangles.

5. Opportunities Driven by Events

Corporate Actions: Keep an eye on corporate happenings such product launches, mergers and acquisitions, earnings releases, and alliances. Good news or advancements have the power to move stocks and present trading opportunities.

Sector Rotation: Determine which sectors or industries are seeing a shift in interest from investors. Invest money in industries with room to grow or with a strong sense of the market.

6. Position Sizing and Risk Management

Diversification: To disperse risk and improve overall portfolio stability, diversify your investments among a range of asset classes, industries, and investing methods.

Position Sizing: Steer clear of overinvesting in stale stocks. Depending on your risk tolerance, your portfolio goals, and the state of the market as a whole, choose the right position sizes.

7. Constant Observation and Modification

Keep Yourself Informed: Keep an eye on macroeconomic variables that may affect stock prices as well as market movements, economic data, and corporate news.

Adapt Strategies: Show flexibility by modifying your trading or investing plans in response to fresh data, shifting market dynamics, and emerging opportunities.

8. Make Use of Expert Advice

Financial Advisors: For individualized advice, investment recommendations, and risk management techniques, speak with seasoned financial advisors, investment specialists, or portfolio managers.

Using a combination of fundamental analysis, income generation tactics, technical analysis, event-driven possibilities, and active monitoring can increase the possibility for returns in a sideways market, even if benefitting from stationary stocks needs patience, vigilance, and risk management. It's critical to match investment techniques to your time horizon, investment goals, and risk tolerance. You should also think about getting professional counsel as necessary.

In summary:

A variety of factors, such as geopolitical events, investor sentiment, company performance, and economic conditions, have shaped the stock market's dynamic fluctuations. To sum up the stock market, consider these important points:

Market Volatility: There have been times when there has been a lot of movement in the stock market, including bull markets and bear markets. Global events, the publication of economic data, changes in investor mood, and central bank policy have all contributed to fluctuations.

Performance of Sectors: Some sectors have performed better than others. One such industry is technology, which has advanced in e-commerce, cloud computing, artificial intelligence, and digital transformation. With an emphasis on drugs, biotechnology, and telemedicine, healthcare also had a big impact, particularly during the COVID-19 pandemic.

Investor techniques: A variety of techniques have been used by investors, such as technical analysis, growth, value, and dividend investing. Amidst market volatility, risk management, asset allocation, and long-term investing goals have been critical factors to take into account.

Market Participants: Algorithmic trading platforms, hedge funds, institutional investors, and retail investors have all influenced market dynamics. Online trading platforms have enabled more engagement from regular investors, which has affected stock movements and market sentiment.

Worldwide Factors: The success of the stock market has been influenced by global economic trends, trade dynamics, geopolitical conflicts, and regulatory changes. The phenomenon of global market interconnectivity has resulted in cross-regional correlations and spillover effects.

The future direction of the economy, inflationary pressures, interest rate policies, geopolitical threats, corporate earnings growth, and technology breakthroughs continue to influence the stock market outlook. While navigating market risks and uncertainties, investors keep evaluating opportunities.

In general, the stock market depicts a dynamic setting where risks and possibilities coexist. Investors must use prudent investment methods, diligent research, risk management techniques, and market trend awareness to successfully navigate and seize opportunities in the stock market.

www.ingramcontent.com/pod-product-compliance
Lightning Source LLC
Chambersburg PA
CBHW082358220526
45470CB00008B/2786